DO UNLOVE TO LOVE

Priyashruthi Sivasankar

"We always need to be unloved, to feel what it is to be loved."

CONTENTS

IS IT JUST ME?
HUMBLY HAUNTED
I'M SCARED
I'M BLUNTLY HATED
I CAN'T HANDLE THIS
HURT LESS-HATE MORE
IS EVERYTHING FINE?
ALL ABOUT MINE

HAPPILY NEVER AFTER

THE STUPID POEMS

I always dreamt about creating wonders
Lying on a broken stone bench.
I remember crying over my biggest blunders
Struggling to swallow my lunch.

It was a year ago, but it feels like ages
When I addressed him with that name.
I don't hold any remorseful regrets,
To have been everything that is lame.

I didn't see through when I met him
Nor did I expect to softly succumb.
But I realized I am no one to him
To have written all the stupid poems.

I have always been an unsaid torture
That he had to shoo away.
But he let me put myself in order,
And call him any day.

He is not just a character in my stories
But the start of everything.
He exists only in my theories
That I could loudly sing

I didn't want to bother him
Nor did I expect any of it to come.
But he knew I had built a whole realm
To have treasured all the stupid poems.

Pen and paper
In the dusty air.
I have never heard
The first word
For any of the stupid poems.

I am tired
As they said
"You cling
On to nothing
Through the stupid poems."

I didn't know anything about him
Nor did I choose to learn him.
But I know I did my maximum
To throw away all the stupid poems.

URSULA AGAIN

The music in my head rises
And I turned on all the vices
That I hid inside my head.
I stop myself from earning praises,
And choose to sulk in your gazes.
I unread all the stories I read.

I think about all the "what ifs"
Refuse to see the "buts"
Though I know all the hiccups
Something stops me from giving up.

I am Ursula again
Falling for Ariel's Eric again
I am vicious when it's love.
Scorned, since the vow

I never loved him in my vein
But I wanted to be a princess again.
It was easy for them to make me a witch.
I could escape this terrible pain
Only when I completely gain
The prince, who could save me from this glitch.

So, I am Ursula again
Falling for Ariel's Eric again
I am vicious when it's love.
Scorned, since the vow

But, slowly, I see us together,
And wonder why I bother
To call off all my masterplan?
It would still be a smolder
To lean on his shoulder
And rule back my clan

I atleast got myself back in this love affair.
I atleast get someone to share
All the grief that made me a ugly
Witch, who can also be lovely.

I atleast find someone on land.
I atleast set myself in the grand
Which I lost to my own brother
Cursed to die alone in the farther

Why does he not mean anything he says?
In all the so-called assumed clues
I am hoping for him to love me
But, Ariel it is, I see.

I'm just realizing it is not him that I should win.
I'm just realizing it is me who I should not succumb
To escape my harsh reality
Of being a witch and suffer honestly.

And, I am Ursula again
Trying to see beyond the line
I am vicious when it's love.
Scorned, since the vow

IN THE WONDERLAND

She was so taken away
Until she saw what flew away.
Her friends and cousins
Listed down his sins.

And she didn't know how to make up her mind
'Cause she had already fallen deep.
She didn't know how she let herself be blind
Until she fell through the leap.

Into the wonderland, where he was the hero.
Into the wonderland, where she heard only him on her
stereo.

She was swirled
By how much he thrilled
Her with his subtle smile
That she couldn't afford to see, even for a while

She now blamed herself
To have lost the potential in nobody.
What if the conflict is herself?
And she chooses to burn her body.

No one cared to see through her
And she chose not to as well.
She waited for him to be aware
That she heard voices from inside the well.
She lost herself in the woods
To find what she has got.
She drowned herself deep in his roots
And found what she has lost.

In the wonderland, where he held her hostage

In the wonderland, where he treasured his tales from the
Stone Age.

He has got nothing to lose
He has his subjects, who are all fools.
She thought they were inseparable
But she realized it was all despicable.
She found her door out
And paved her own route.

She didn't need anyone
To find her way to her heart
She just had to have a little burn down
To make sense even in her blurts.

In the wonderland, where he was an outsider
In the wonderland, where he was a little nicer.

US, IN MY STORY SCRIPT

"What a desperate bitch"
"With the laughter of an evil witch?"
Did you hear those echoes
From your stupid fellows?
Did I ever tell you why I glitch?

'Cause I see many worlds in my mind.
And I try to blend and grind
Every instance I see and didn't see
I chose not to heal
I am very good at faking a smile.
I forgot what is real and my lie

You were one of those "my lies"
Which made me realize I am wise.
If I want, I can sketch a plan
And win you into my clan.
But I am a woman with defined dreams
And I hope you never hear my screams.
'Cause whoever I write about
Never learn what is in my heart.

We never give each other a shit
You can't come close to me, even a bit.
There is a huge line that will split
Us, in my story script.

Have I ever told you
That I enjoy being blue?
There are times
When there is no reason for my whines.
I stick to sadness with glue.

But you deserve all the happiness.

So, I left you entirely clueless.
I saw a future together
With the good and bad, altogether.
You bring a smile to my face
With no effort, at an easy pace.
You've shown me that the real world
Is not as crude and bad.

I know you don't even listen
And you don't care if my words glisten.
We crave different worlds
And I should not slide down from gold.
I wish we could be this way
Even when I fly away,
'Cause whoever I write about
Never learn what is in my heart.

Have I ever told you that you can win the world?
Maybe not the entire world, but whatever is being sold.
'Cause there is not a bit
Of us, in my story script.

I wonder if I ever spoke to you, apart
From the "us" in my story script.

SAD SONG

I hear the clock go tick-tock
I hear my heart racing hard
Wanting to do something that means more
Like building our evermore

I'm afraid I'll be used to this routine
Of doing nothing between 9 and 5.
I feel like a cheap sixteen
Who acts stupid and naive.

"I hope to see you sometime soon."
I always say this to the moon.
Hoping the message reaches you someday,
And since then, I'll stop walking alone.

I'm afraid I'll settle for less,
Or choose to fall off and roll down the staircase.
I'm talking shit to entertain
The whole room with people who are uncertain.

Sad song,
I feel like a sad song.
Sad song,
That was never sung.

You feel so indifferent from the whole world
Something more special and close to my heart.

I want to build memories with you
Break the buttons and slowly sew.
Love letters and photographs that we preserve
And, the rest, our love serves.

I'm afraid I might give up
From wanting to be unconditionally in love.

I think at midnight
About all our unarmed fights.

Sad song,
We feel like a sad song.
Sad song,
That I always listen.

We feel so different from the whole world
Something more special and close to my heart.

SCARECROW YOU'VE NEVER SEEN

The thought of you not being mine
Doesn't really sadden me.
I thought I would end up crying with white wine
While watching, you happily flee.

I am not healthy.
My thoughts are filthy.
I oversee,
And I over fee.l
I would've been
A scarecrow you've never seen.

I sit here all alone,
Waiting for you to magically show up.
Though I know you go
To the other store for your coffee sip.
Still, I want to show you where I am from,
And where I grew up.

I am searching for your pale shirt,
And I am struggling not to blurt
This weird complex
Niche that I unapologetically flex.
Our eyes speak
Whatever we seek,
The intriguing intimacy
That speaks purity.

I think a lot about you on this trip.
I spoke about you while playing poker.
I never imagined the tables would flip,
That I would suddenly feel like a joker

The intrusive thoughts
Causes all the holocausts

That haunts
The beautiful icks
About love shifts
From right chests to wrong wrists.

I might hold your neck under a knife,
And threaten you to say 'love of my life'.
I am afraid I'll scare you,
And regret it after you flew.
Anyway, I don't enjoy what I've been,
A scarecrow you've never seen

I am not sure.
If I am that unworthy of the allure,
If I'll ever cure
The mind that is impure,
And it's an undeserving heart that is pure.
I'm afraid to say 'forever.'
Will I ever heal, like ever?

I see you walking down the hallway,
And not feel the same anymore
Why was it this easy anyway?
Maybe I found myself right away.
After I learnt, you were sure
To shoo me far away
Like everyone who has been
In my life, a scarecrow you've never seen.

Did I scare you?
'Cause I see you unsee through
The empty room of memories.
As if we danced around the trees.
I wish I could see what you've seen.
A scarecrow you've never seen.

DESCRIBE YOU

I win each game against you,
But you won my heart with no due.
It is imperfect
That makes me want to trust
That is how it is,
A strategic bliss.

I am struggling to stop writing about you.
With all the words I know,
I want to describe the lifeful you.
I want us to grow in this flow.
My playlist suddenly screams your name.
I want to give up
My thirst for fortune and fame.
For your sake, I might want to live up.

Does our vibe really match?
It doesn't matter behind the locked latch
Of my shattered heart,
Which I picked from the lottery lot.
I can't tell you I love you,
But you look like my beautiful blue.

I read you like I read a book.
And I know all that you've shown.
Now I want us to walk down the brooke.
You have faded off the moon,
And I hate you for that.
By the thought of you, I am bereaved.
You are good enough to reconstruct
All the things that I unbelieved.

I am dying to break this language
To describe you as a fancy package.

There is no real man who has made me
Want to see, feel, and grieve.
You made me easily unarmed,
And entered my heart unalarmed.
To plant the seed of reality,
And teach me some clarity.

I know it is never happening,
But I keep telling the same to jinx for the worse.
It is very concerning
How much I am consumed when you are close.
I will come running to your home
Breathing my lungs out,
To describe you as what I have won.
I don't mind even if I pass out.

I MUST'VE BEEN NUTS

SHAME ON ME

It's something about him
That I can't forget.
It has always been about the win
Myself, I wouldn't forgive.

I remember,
How he made it safe
Like a sweet embrace.
Now, I'm in disgrace.
Shame on me,
I remember
Erasing the trace.
Now, I recollect the phrase.
"I don't fit in the maze."
Shame on me.

The wedding return gift,
The diary which was green.
I think I'm not over it yet,
I still write about him.

I remember,
"It is all in your wit,
You've got all the right
To blindly ink it."
Shame on me.
I remember
How unafraid I was
To show all my flaws.
Now, I can't hear his applause.
Shame on me.

I think this will be done
Only when I find someone.
He plays a major role

Then I summed up on the pole.
Someone calls me delusional,
That I am incapable.
I look back on "the twelve days".
Now I don't find myself in that place.

I remember,
How supportive they were,
How he loved to care
And anything I could share.
Shame on me.
I remember,
How big my smile was
Through all those days.
I should've dropped my ways.
Shame on me .

AND WHATNOT

I ask that mediocre
Girl who calls herself a writer
To write about us
And how we were done and dusted.

She warned me a hundred times
That you've got no spines
To say what you show
And be carried away in the flow.

Everything felt so fresh.
I felt you one bit less
Every single day
Since you chose to walk away.

I thought I knew you well enough,
Imagining your times were rough.
Well, what about mine?
You ended up being my parade rain
'Cause I still hope
That we pull each other with a rope.

It really makes me sad
That you are not doing good
I wish I could talk to your dad.
And set you free to be glad.
Why did we say that
In our late night chat?
Why did we even do that
When we decide not to fight the combat?

Flowers, leaves, and bracelets,
And what not we give each other?
Tears, playlists, and regrets,
And whatnot, we didn't tell each other.

Smiles, grins, and teeth
And whatnot, we showed each other
Love, trust, and faith
And whatnot did we hide from each other?

I'm not sorry
To have left you in your worry,
In times when you need someone.
'Cause, it's high time I saw mine.

I quite remember the first time
When we felt the red line,
That we thought intertwined.
Besides how the stars align
To mislead us to different line,
And remind it is just fine
Even when we are not the same,
We would at least be sane.

SPIRAL WHEELS

I hear the chorus
Like in the fancy old churches
Of our parable, it has no end or beginning.
I feel you are a lesson of my "story London"
And I will pray for you to God, the father and son.

Because, I lifted
My long dropped head
To just look into those wide eyes.
And I look back and wonder, "how time flies."
'Cause I'm falling out
Or whatever we could call it.

Now, I feel sane
And I slow down to the sideline
To look in the mirror and talk to myself.
'Cause I will never tell you how I feel
About you, and leave us in a spiral wheel.

Because, I have been
Through this when I was a teen.
I will be left with nice poems,
But it will also shatter my realms
That I have built for my crown.
You are capable of leaving it in ruin.

Because, I have seen
The falling bridge in London,
And it took a lot of embarrassing efforts
To earn back my guts,
To not float on air,
When I assume we both are a pair.

Now, I am clear

Of what to bear
In my malfunctioning mind.
'Cause I will never tell you how I feel
About you, and leave us in a spiral wheel

I see us in America,
In a studio apartment,
Making coffee mocha,
In love, with no amendment.
You are no replica
Of the characters in my mut.

Now, I know more
About how to escape offshore
As the right time hits, I leave you with hints.
'Cause I will never tell you how I feel
About you, and leave us in a spiral wheel

LETHALLY TIRED

It has been a month since he came back
Back on a vacation.
I prayed I would never get to see him again.
But I also hoped that we crossed paths
Crossed paths sporadically again,
And clear the void and not hang on.

I don't know him anymore
As if I did before.
Don't know what has gone sour
As if I did before.

I truly hope that I have already moved on,
And figured what happens next and so on.
'Coz I am lethally tired.
I thought I knew that we weren't meant to be.
What did I even fail to see?
Maybe I was lethally tired.

What am I waiting for?
Why do I even care?
Even after a long year,
Why do I even care?

I just wish I had made it to that birthday party,
Birthday party in a busy city.
I would have had a great time.
Not just because he wouldn't be tartly,
But to prove my clear shore and fidelity.
A glass of wine should be fine.

I truly hope that I don't sound hopeful,
Or like a clingy fool.
'Cause I am lethally tired.
It's just he instigated my intrinsic insecurity

That I have no redeeming quality.
Maybe I was lethally tired.

I don't know him anymore
As if I did before.
Don't know what has gone sour
As if I did before.

I truly hope that he doesn't get to read this,
Or even see me in his peripheral mist
'Cause I am lethally tired.
I don't want to pull this grim topic out.
Can't face another one-sided drought.
'Cause I am legally tired.

What am I waiting for?
Why do I even care?
Even after a long year,
Why do I even care?

I NEVER THOUGHT

I never thought I would be burnt down
In your sweet summer arson.

I knew I was not the only one,
But it is strange that I knew she was the other.
There is something between me and her.
We are each other's spur.

It happened in the same fucking day.
We both chose to ignore it anyway.
I've already been there
Receiving intense glare,
But I never heard a voice.
"You were never a choice"
I know you would claim,
And I would end up in shame

I never thought I would write about you and me.
I hide all of these poems under your sleeve.

I know you are better than
A lot of other men.
I think, all my plans
Would work like my pen.
But I don't want to
Win you and make you mine.
You deserve more than two
You deserve to shine.

I'd miss all those signs

You gave me unapologetically.
I'd miss your glance
You gave me intensely.
I'd miss the silly prince
You were when you see me.

I never thought I would be burnt down
In your sweet summer arson.

Anything that is meant to be
Will find its way to me.
I don't want to care about you,
But I fight myself not look at you.

I did it another time
Like I owned your time.
I never thought I would be burnt down
In your sweet summer arson.

I DID ALL THAT I DID

I am running back and forth
To home and you.
To learn if it is all worth
To keep you in due.

The moment I saw your face,
The moment I realized you are what I had to face,
That instance, I had to handle what was real.
That instance, I had to feel fear.

I know this isn't love
Just like I always did.
But now I wonder how
I did all that I did.

I shamelessly cried in front of you.
I seamlessly smiled at you.
I hardly looked away from you.
I effortlessly learnt your habits.
I spoke out all my second thoughts.
I feel all of these are for the worst.

You bought my book
But never cared to open it.
Just like anyone I look
And pretend to befriend shit.

I know this isn't love.
Just like I always did.
But now I wonder how
I did all that I did.

The moment you saw me,
The moment you were forced to know me,
The instance you ever read this,

The instance when you know I felt the "us".

You'll know that I also knew
That we were one of those cursed few,
Who could never be anything true,
But just look at each other,
And avoid hurting one another.
We were never meant to be forever.

I believe in things that never fit.
You do believe in the same shit,
That I have done for years now.
I am amazed somehow
When you speak my mind.
And I did all that I did.

I wish we were in a different universe
Where everything can be at ease,
Where I would've had the courage
To speak up for what I feel without any budge.

I wish I had never done all that I did.
I wish I had handled it with more secrecy,
Given that I had learnt a lesson previously.
But I did all that I did.

ALL OVER AGAIN

I thought we were over
For a number of times.
I thought I was done with you.
I stood there under the shower
Recalling my whines.
I didn't plan to give you a clue.

I should never drink gin tonic again.
I don't have the tolerance for the pain
That will be caused
By my words, that was boozed.

I am totally intoxicated
By your laughter that I said I hated,
Like it was all fine
In your bloody mind.

But I don't know why I can't skip this spiral,
Be dead by the revival.
I blame myself all over again.
But I don't know why I can't hear your denial
Before I chose to drink and dial.
I blame myself all over again.

I wasn't wise enough.
I shouldn't have pinned the blondie.
It would've been better if I had passed out,
Than say things that would be tough,
And familiarize your hobby
When you daringly chill out.

I wouldn't say I was jealous,
But I can't either be selfless.
I am no saint.
I wish I could keep you hostage.

With all my discovered and preserved courage
My only real paint.

But I don't know why I shy away and act weird
When you are around.
I blame myself all over again.
But I don't know why I act like a coward
In this meaningless crowd.
I blame myself all over again.

But I don't know why I keep jumping back
Knowing this glass will always have a crack.
I blame myself again
But I don't know why you listen to my bark
In dark midnight black.
But still, I blame myself again.

DESPERATE DEVIL

DO I EVEN KNOW YOU?

I thought I would be fine
When everything falls in line.
Everyone is glad for me
And I'm sad that you don't see.

I am trying to hold hope
Before it slithers off the rope.
I have surrendered
Thinking love will turn red.

How do I make up for all my mistakes in between?
I can't assure you, in reality, that my head is clean.
How do I make myself seen,
In your blindspot vision?
But, I'd also ask where you have been?

Do you see that I'm waiting for you?
Have you read what I wrote for you?
Do you even know I love you?
I can't really hold it
Knowing at every step that I'm losing it.
Do I even know you?

I regret settling for reality
Which is not very pretty.
Everyone is ready to hunt
But victory is just a stunt.

I can't put up with people
Who aren't hopeful
About finding their way
Through this tough game.

How else do I make my way to you

When the crowd has poisoned me blue?
By giving no clue
How do I sue
Them for all the words they've used?

Do you know that I'm suffering without you?
Do you read what I write to you?
Do you even know I love you?
I can't really hold it
Knowing at every step that I'm losing it.
Do I even know you?

I thought I had achieved something huge,
But they pulled my tail to be a refugee.
From my castle top
To the matrix loop,
I'm struggling to breathe
Even on an open heath.

I thought I was a warrior
A savior, a mother.
Who is strong and loved
I realized I was nothing but a joke.
A choke, a broke
Who is weak and trolled.

Do you know that I'm nothing without you?
Do you read what I write to you?
Do you even know I love you?
I can't really hold it
Knowing at every step that I'm losing it.
Do I even know you?

DO CARE

He was my only story,
A tale with no glory.
He was 25 years old.
So, he obviously knew more.

I was a sad burden.
Nothing could worsen.
I was 20 years old.
So, I didn't want more.

I am considering flying to his town,
Ready to fantasize about being a clown.
I crave some positivity
That I can't find in this cruel city.

Will he even care to save me from this crisis?
How do I describe what this feeling is?
I think about him when they break me into pieces.
He taught me what mind cease is.

Does he even care?
About what I write, with all right
Should he even care?
About my plight, and torn kite
Why do I care?
About his flight, with the whites

He had all the fun
That I hated a ton.
Did he throw a glance
At any of my plans?

I wanted to be better,
Better than his future.
Everytime I wanted to win,

Anywhere more than him,

I would lose miserably and run back to him,
Attempting to commit the same stupid sin.
But I was rather in safe hands.
He taught me what trust was.

But, does he even care?
About what I write, with all right
Should he even care?
About my plight, and torn kite
Why do I care?
About his flight, with the whites

I wish I could talk to him once more
In the dark monsoon pour.
To ask what his kindness is for
From his inner core.

I hope he remembers me,
Or how he let me be,
And set me free
Everytime he sees the sea.

Does he even care?
About what I write, with all right
Should he even care?
About my plight, and torn kite
Why do I care?
About his flight, with the whites

OTHERWISE, JUST LIKE THE WISE

I would like to tell you
That I know you know.
We leave each other in blurred hue,
And take it with the flow.

You act weird. Every now and then,
Your shield goes up and down.
I wonder if it has something to do with her.
I had no idea we'd go this far.

I hear your fake laughter,
And how you hope for me to save you.
I see it in your bloody eyes,
That screams "I know I am in there
In your lines with all due
Respect, I know all your lies."

I thought I would easily escape
As there is nothing to escalate.
But you think otherwise
We don't say but hint, just like the wise.

I am the bestest woman
You have ever met.
I have deeply sowen
The idea of "no love, I bet".

Because I worry if it'd be you
That comes in all my tarot cards.
I don't want you to be the "you",

Also I hate when someone plays hard.

I hear your thoughts
They scream my name too loud.
I usually do it.
Leaving men in the haunts.
I am a little proud
That I never fit

In any of your little world
Where everyone is shrewd.
But you think otherwise
We don't say but hint, just like the wise.

I want to go back to the love of my life,
But I could never be the suitor for the wife.
This is so harsh on me
I would rather die in the tsunami.
And I want you to know
When you ever get to know,

I hear your silence
That says "don't come near me".
I might have sacred you
With my demons and weapons.
I just want you to flee
And find the right one for you.

Maybe I was wrong all along.
Only in my stories, you might belong.
But you think otherwise
We don't say but hint, just like the wise.

THIS ISN'T LOVE

He is doing perfectly fine.
Actually, I ain't sure.
It has been a long time,
And I failed the closure.

A few weeks ago
I wish I had met him.
And took it slow
Not like a rash on the skin.

I sit in a room full of boys,
And narrate how much he loved Lego toys.
I know this isn't love.
'Cause I don't remember his voice,
And clearly, I was never his choice.
I know this isn't love.

But, to win his heart
I have one sweet sweep
I have been lying that
I didn't have any hope.
I hoped he played his part
Like a dream in my sleep.
Is it an assault?
That I hold some hope.

He is private
So I hear no news.
I can't hold a secret
I let everything loose.

Sometimes I'm angry,
My face turns red,
'Cause he doesn't ping me.
He didn't want me to be misled.

I sit in a room full of boys,
Dead in silence,
There's no noise.
I know this isn't love.
None of these were my choice.
I try hard to be poised.
I know this isn't love.

But to forget him
With no effort,
I have been trying hard
To hold on and have hope.
I narrate him like a film
With details on his shirt.
I fancily said
"I didn't have any hope."

Everyday I choose to forget him.
Shamelessly I end up writing about him.
Boiling a bottle of gin,
Knowing he doesn't give a damn about what I write.
So I took all the liberty and right,
In owning our story and my plight.

I remember him,
And the memories
That made me say,
"I didn't have any hope."
I let everyone win,
And try to live properly.
To build my own way,
That needs only hope.

WHAT ARE WE?

I am stuck in a dim city,
And I feel extremely guilty
For a lot of things that I ruined.
I have been trying my best
To get some mental rest.
It's you, look at who I have found.

I sit idly for five hours straight.
For something to build dramatically
It has been three months, a long wait.
I laugh at you hysterically.
We both make everything light.
But not the things that have to be treated carefully.

What are we, when we can live in shacks
With the utmost ease?
I never thought about this.
What are we, when we fill what the other lacks?
I am warm and you freeze
And we are equally capable cheats.

This is too soon.
Just like how it has been,
A couple of long years ago.
This ain't intoxicating,
And we ain't working.
But, I am trying hard not to have hope.

Again, I don't want to cry for anyone,
Who is aiming to not feel not won.
I hope I can be two people.
So, living in both worlds is feasible.
Things are going out of hand.
'Cause I have set all my plans

On point, and you enter out of nowhere.
And broke it in a simple stare.

What are we, if I don't know
Your mother's name?
And you say the same.
What are we, when there is more
Than this silly game,
And a photo frame?

No one should ever know your name.
It is better to kill your character right away.
It does slightly hurt me
To choose to live in glory
Of being a righteous woman
And be swept from the feet by a man
Who I have never imagined?
And I am dying with this guilt.

What are we when you do the same?
To live the structure
And have you planned your future?
What are we if we can never blame
Anyone for this torture
Which screams luster?

CAN YOU

No matter what I do,
I feel like I dwell in a zoo
With beasts around me
Ravenous to kill and eat.

They say I don't belong here.
It justifies that they didn't hear.
My tear's howl to come
Out of this dark room.

I don't blame anyone for being quiet.
But for me to understand, they have to say it.
No face here feels like home.
I go back to my room.
Through the window I see the moon,

I ask, can you see,
I ask, can you hear,
I beg to escape these
And live with no fear.

No matter what I do
I struggle here with no clue.
How can I set myself free?
When I can't find ways to flee.

One says how to hold on to it,
With his miserable story bit.
He has been through a hard time,
But he smiles and does not whine.

I don't know if I am happy or sad.
I am doing fine, but I can't be glad.
You are my only home.

Now I am dying from being alone.
I want to be with you before our time is gone.

I ask, can you see,
I ask, can you hear,
I beg to escape these
And live with no fear.

There are too many men around
Who tells me what is my paramount?
They try to bring out the worst me
And show some sympathy.
To play the victimized heroes,
By being my valued foe,
I am faking that I've got nothing,
By pretending something.

HUG ME TIGHT

You, my Sun, moved North.
A new age henceforth.
I didn't know if that would ever stop.
Deprived of the warmth,
And synthetic strength
I didn't know if I would ever cope.

I now play all the rotten, swallowed promises.
I cry, not knowing whether love is true or false.
Will they ever talk to me, to my face?
Will I ever get to you at this pace?

Hug me tight when I get to you there.
Hug me tight till my muscles wither and tear.
I hope they understand that you are my only desire.
Hug me tight like it's all over.

I searched the whole world
Couldn't find a piece of gold.
I now know how to not give up.
I froze in summer snow
I didn't know why I did so.
I now know how to hold hope.

You are the James Quinn piece that brings my smile.
But to hear that I have been waiting a long while.
The moment I think you've gone out of sight,
You turn in and throw a shine.
Bright like I should stop whining,
And not look for the ending,
Until your homecoming,
And our bright mornings.

I now think of all the omens, unmarked signals.
I always wondered about broken crystals.

Will they ever stop showing faces?
Will I ever get to solve all the mazes?

Hug me tight when I get to you there.
Hug me tight till my muscles wither and tear.
I know sometimes I get crazy and bizarre.
Hug me tight like it's all over.

THIS & THAT

"SORRY"

November rain
Partially dissolved my pain.
But all over again,
The emotional drain.

Lost myself in the love-sick crowd.
Lost my pride to the man who is always proud.
None of them intended to be shrewd.
But, I was maimed, just for the record.

Trying to regain
All the long-lost shine.
I try hard to align,
And bring back my reign.

I don't recall what we were,
All the food and jokes we shared,
The weight that they made me bear.
That is all I remember.
The simple word, "sorry"
And that solves all the grit between us.
Me saying that sorry
And they don't realize what they did for once.
Just the word, sorry
Is it worth all the second chances?

Sometimes I feel like it's high time
To cut out and start again.
With the same people
But a different plot line.

I blinded my eyes and passed on.
I freeze my feelings to move on.
On my guilt parade, they showered rain.
They are worth all the pain in my veins.

Loved myself in the love-sick crowd.
I found my worth from the man who is always proud.
It was fun solving the feud.
And, I love them, just for the record.

The simple word, "sorry"
And that solves all the grit between us.
Me saying that sorry
And they need not realize what they did for once.
Just the word, "sorry"
It might be worth all the chances.

Still, I would kill some characters happily
Drinking tanqueray and martini,
When I get lost and lonely.
When I get lost and lonely,
I sing and dance wistfully
To the songs I used to listen merrily

So I feel the simple word, "sorry"
Should not be the reason for us.
Just the word "sorry"
Should never be the reason for us.

HIGH AND PAIN

Everyone roots for us
But I have to give us some space.
'Cause the moment I saw you
With that immense focus,
I knew you had your own ways,
And enjoy giving the trickiest clues.
For a moment I had to sit
And think what is it?

'Cause I bluntly feel the high.
What the fuck did you mean by
"For once and forever."
When you know what lies after?
'Cause I bluntly feel the pain,
When I had to say "I am the Abel for your Cain"
Because I see it in your eyes
When we deliberately say those lies.
I bluntly feel the high and pain.
I bluntly can't be the Abel for your Cain.

A hundred reasons build
For me to fall apart and rebuild.
I sit looking in your direction.
I want to carry the guilt
Again, like in the era of the cult.
But I can't take another rejection.
For a moment I had to sit
And think what is it?

'Cause I bluntly feel the high
You don't feel like someone who just passes by.
Like it hasn't always been
In your eyes I feel seen.
I bluntly feel the pain.

'Cause I know we shall never dance in the rain.
Then why this electric josh?
I wish I could find what I lost.
I bluntly feel the high and pain.
I bluntly want to dance with you in the rain.

I don't feel any silly thing
For you in my broken heart.
But I'm in the verge of asking
You out to the Walmart.
I know this isn't love
Like in the classic movies.
But we clearly outdrove
All the signs we should've seen.
We feel the high and land in pain.
By all the signs we should've seen.

'Cause we bluntly feel the high,
But we choose to live the lustrous lie.
What would it be if it was us?
Would there be something more than lust?
We bluntly feel the pain.
'Cause we can not walk the same line.
Did you see what I saw?
Something in my eyes, something raw.
We bluntly feel the high and pain.
Can't we bluntly be one and walk the same line?

DID YOU OR AM I?

I see people in love,
And think "how?"
I haven't felt it my whole life.
Is it even true?
With fancy colors they drew
The portrait of cupid, but it is a lie.

What if you were asked to write about me?
I'm curious what you've seen
All this time, in this brief time.
You never seemed interested or keen.
But still, I hate to keep it all clean,
When you give me those signs, those silly signs.

Did you ever give me those signs,
Or am I just making up these lines?
Maybe I am out of things to write.
So the peripheral characters are now bright.
Shining so bright,
That I never let you wait
And make sure you don't escape this bait.
This non bailable bait.
Intoxicating ourselves in white wine,
And dancing in the midnight rain.

It was special
When we twinned for real,
And had a simple dinner.
In the corner of my head
You are signaling red.
I wondered if you liked me or her.

We act like we are lost in the keith.
But also say, "Only us, shall we?"

I hate to say it, but I truly consider
Us to make it through
All the faces those aren't true,
And live a life that is better, even worse.

Did you ever give me those signs,
Or am I just making up these lines?
'Cause sometimes you feel real,
And I call you with so much zeal.
The very next moment I feel
Distant and unseen.
You could treat me like a queen,
Or leave me unseen.
I sit alone and dine,
Thinking if you are doing fine.

What if I tell you that I feel this way?
I've done this already anyway.
I know, it hurts for a while,
But you are not the one in the aisle.
So, it is fine to keep it to myself,
And hide your character on the shelf,
And never feel you in my skin,
And let the love overflow over the rim.
But you come back with that eye smile,
So I let it all be, for a while.

Did you ever give me those signs,
Or am I making up these lines?
It just starts as doubt,
"Am I falling in or out?"
When you recall your early youth
Will you remember us and our half-baked truth?
And how we were,
When it was dark in there,
How you appreciate what I wear,

How I dive into your soul with just a glare,
And how you replied with a side stare.
Maybe you were never aware.

SORRY AGAIN

He is back in town,
And I act like I didn't care.
I feel like a foolish clown
Whenever I can't describe what we were.

I can't unweed him from my head,
As I am just out of things to write.
Now I just lie on my bed
And think if I was right.

I think about him for hours
The same way as dying flowers.
Or hold his memories tight
And give up the fight.
Or just wait for some light.

Am I sorry again?
So, was I at sorry back then
Ah! sorry again, I was sorry then.

I climb up high
With one leg on his shoulder ready to fall.
I can see how he sighed
Everytime I baselessly called.

Something in me just
Asked me to call it off.
In my emotional burst
He stood there stiff .

I should've left it right there.
I don't like the fact that I dared.
I feel enraged.
I ended up being bizarre
'Coz I held him hostage.

Am I sorry again?
So was I at sorry back then
Ah! sorry again, I was sorry then.

He was gone
Quite far long.
I failed to chase him with
My stupid songs.

I hate that I'm the one at sympathy,
He remained a mystery,
That I failed to see.
Because that's how he wanted it to be.

Maybe we weren't bound to be.
Does he even think about me?
Or care about my burnt strategy?
I shouldn't have written any.

Am I sorry again?
So was I at sorry back then
Ah! sorry again, I was sorry then.

PARADOX

I commit all the sins
And wait for a frog prince,
To break the spell
And leave me in the dark well.

I sometimes think that I am content,
But otherwise I expect to be validated
From people around me who I resent
To just not feel isolated.

I am a living paradox
Whose stories are stored in the box
As bedtime stories for my children.
In the process I become my own burden.
I have to unlove the old me
To discover and find the true me.

I break all my planned virtues.
I kill myself to not be one of the trues.
That fits in any of their factory
That produces slaves for no territory.

I sometimes think I am absolutely fine,
And I realize I don't have any courage.
So, the very moment I end up crying,
And give up jumping off and fight with rage.

I am a living paradox
I hunt for myself like a cunning fox,
And also cry for being the loved one,
For literally no one
In this whole wide world.
I feel like I am always tortured.

Why do I wait for a prince?

Why can't I rinse all of my sins
Through the beginning, middle and end?
I'd unlove and start afresh and not blend.

I fooled myself by blaming the time,
Thinking throughout that I was fine.
I learnt to stop myself from crossing the line.
I should just be the Abel for his Cain.

I am a living paradox
Who sleeps, walks and slowly trots
In worlds that don't exist.
I try hard between persist and resist.

I am a living paradox
Who keeps it low and flaunts.
Who loves and hates the prison.
Who shatters and glues what I've written.

IS IT JUST ME?

We can be a part of different teams.
We might have our own flying fleets.
I feel like a four petal clover,
And I feel like a blooming flower.

I don't know what to call you
When I am annoyed by how much I admire you.
I don't know what to do
When I am stuck in the same elevator as you.

Is it just me,
Who is feeling all of these?
Is it just me,
Who is able to feel
All the tension when we are alone?
All the comfort even when we are not friends?
I dared to chug the bottle of liquor
Because I should stop precisely by the threads,
That I had written in my script.
You are just the supporting character.
And the heroine has all the grit
To try something better.

So she walks to you
And says it all like a fool
Not knowing what you'd say.
Who cares, it is just a play.
Will you take her or be furious?
I am just curious.

I don't know how to end it.
Would you love her, sing and dance in the rain?
I don't know if you feel it.
Would you say 'no' and leave her in quailing pain?

Is it just me
Who is glorifying nothing?
Is it just me
Who is exaggerating?

All the stupid stop signs,
Are they even real?
All the useless pass times,
Are they even real?
I am dying to touch you
But I wonder if you are real.
I am dying to feel me in you,
But I ask if you are real.

I have seen you close by
But is that real?
I have talked to you for a while
Is that even real?
I admire your lashes
They are too pretty to be real.
I breathe in your cigar ashes
They are too nice to be real.

You are not so nice,
Which makes you real
Should I just throw the dice,
And test my luck as a deal.

I don't know how to tell you
That I felt too real when you are around me.
I don't know what you are up to
When you act like there is nothing for you to feel.
I don't know what to do
When you don't really see me.
I don't know how to be cool

When you dive into me, when you just see
.
Is it just me who feels all of this?
Is it just me who wants to kill this?
Is it just me or do you also feel this?
Is it just me or do you want to kneel for this curse?

HUMBLY HAUNTED

I'M SCARED

I am scared that I'd give up.
I am scared that I can't live up.

I wish I could go on a long walk
And get some fresh air.
I wish I could have more than a small talk
And try better and harder.
I wish I could unapologetically take a break.
I wish I wasn't a sloppy slack.

I am scared that my tears would dry up.
I am scared that I should rise up.

I wish I could be lost,
And never be found.
I wish I go past
All the reasons that pull me to the ground.
I wish I was not in my miserable past.
I wish I am fighting till the very last.

I live to make up to all my mistakes.
I live to regret all my choices and takes.
Do I have anything to genuinely celebrate?
I keep asking myself,
Why do I decorate my tears on the shelf?
Do I have anything in the future for me to be in such
haste?

I bluntly know that tears are all I have got.
I know that remorse is all life has got.
There is no better beautiful place,
I think of the face behind the plot.
I think of the worst possible shot,
How do I save myself from this dark haze?

I wish I could end my story,
When I cry the last drop of ink.
I wish my family carried no glory.
When I lost my life in a blink
Of a moment that was destined to ruin
Like it was written in old sayings.

If I hadn't wondered
How the world looked
The light, I must've seen.
If I had stayed around,
If I had been heard,
I would've had myself to lean.

I'M BLUNTLY HATED

I feel it in my skin and bones
That I have no one.
I feel it in my heart and head
That I am not appreciated.
I feel it in my body and mind
That there is no point in being kind.

At times I hug myself and cry,
At times I dig myself until my tears dry,
I try hard to put up with this crowd.
But I'm bluntly hated.

At times I wonder why
Can't I pass this hatred by.
I realize I expect to be validated,
And I'm bluntly hated.

I think I'm too much for them.
I should go past the thin.
I think I can't keep up with this team.
I should've been more keen.
I think things have gone out of hands,
There is no point in making fake plans.

In years I suddenly feel tiny as an elf,
In years I feel insecure about myself,
I've struggled to be appreciated.
But I'm bluntly hated.

"You reap what you sow."
Who do I call and cry now?
I look back at nightmares that are faded,
And know that I'm bluntly hated.

They said that I was loud and annoying.
Since I know it, now I'm avoiding.
I wish all the shit were thrown on my face,
I would've handled it with more grace.

I faked my smile line,
Thinking that was enough to put up with the crime.
It's my mistake that I mistook
People liked me at first look.

It was too soon for me to even care,
It was too soon for me to share,
Probably I was sedated,
And now I'm bluntly hated.

All the stories from my dusty diaries
For them, it would be too scary.
I never bothered to translate it,
And now, I'm bluntly hated.

I CAN'T HANDLE THIS

There is no way
That I could forget you,
Or forget everything that I go through.
Behind closed gates,
I know what you both do.
I was someone who trusted you
And was easily fooled
Into your games.

I can't handle it.
Do you even understand?
How do I withstand
All the scars that hurt?
I search for your hand,
And realize it went in sand
I can't handle this.

You knew it all
That I was devoted.
Then how could you be so iron hearted?
You knew it all
That I would be dis-oriented.
But you chose to kill me in flesh and blood.
I bleed our love red,
And choose to fall.

I can't handle it
Do you even understand?
How do I withstand
All the scars that hurt?
I search for your hand,
And found it in his hand
I can't handle this.

Are you happy?

Like you were with me?
I think I know how
To bear it all right now.
But, I still can't handle this.

HURT LESS-HATE MORE

My roar in the warfield
Denying the armor and shield.
I have lost my balance without you.
I chose to embrace the bullets.
I failed to give my fullest.
I can't do this if it wasn't you.

They call this madness a cheap game.
I am fine with taking all the shame,
And owning all the blame.
Because being in love is lame.

I was hoping to hurt you less, less and a little less.
I would rather take all the hate, hate and more hate.

I heard you still defend me,
I heard you still praise me,
You could get away with
All the cheating and scheming,

By saying the things that they did,
By pointing to things I hid.
You could get over with
All the feeling and healing.

Why do you see all the good things?
Why do you not kill all the feelings?
I had no control over what I felt.
Why did I do it knowing I'll be sorry?
Why was I in such a hurry?
I knew you would have it all dealt.

You called me the strong one, but no.
I just don't want to be your foe.
With all my miserable mistakes though,

We could be friends, I still hope.

I was hoping to hurt you less, less and a little less.
I would rather take all the hate, hate and more hate.

I wish I could read the letter book,
I wish I could unpierce the hook,
You can't get away with
That mean taunting and smiling.

I wish you said what they said,
I wish I knew where it all lead,
You can't get over with
All my writing and blighting .

I was hoping to hurt you less, less and a little less.
I would rather take all the hate, hate and more hate.

IS EVERYTHING FINE?

Did she think twice before she did it?
Did she make up her mind for it?
I wonder what was on her head
While writing the poem to call it,
To call him the right fit.
I wonder if she meant it when she said.

"I lost a part of me to you.
In my colorless palette,
You've added all shades of blue."
Why would she even say it,
When she chose to hint with a clue
And kill him alive with it?
Why would she even say it?

"She might have her own reasons."
He has made up his mind in the last 6 months.
He smiles when he quotes her treasons.
He was one of her sinless hunts.
It would take a hundred seasons,
For him to naturally face the fronts.

"I lost a part of me to you.
In my colorless palette,
You've added all shades of blue."
Why would she even say it,
And kill him alive with it?
Why would she even say it?

18 page letters,
Chocolate filled sweaters,
He believed it was for a lifetime.
How could she kill her own line,
And act like everything is fine?
Is everything fine?

Unhealable blisters,
In dying cold winters,
He chose not to see the signs.
He washed all her sins.
And acted like everything is fine.
Is everything fine?

"I lost a part of me to you.
In my colorless palette,
You've added all shades of blue."
Why would she even say it,
When she chose to hint with a clue
And kill him alive with it?
Why would she even say it?

ALL ABOUT MINE

I listen to your "nos" and think,
I listen to all your praises and think,
If I was the one at fault all this time,
Or if you ever lived your life.

I see you being perfect,
I see you being apt,
And wonder to whose rule book,
To fit in whose lookbook.

You never learnt your own feelings.
You never knew what you wanted for yourself.
So you made your life all about mine,
And said it was all fine.

You bought me all the jewels
Made me feel like I was crushing your souls.
By making your life all about mine,
And said it was all fine.

"They say they saw you somewhere,
So don't go anywhere"
You don't bother
To hurt me with the opinions of others.

Why should it matter,
Whatever dying words they wither?
I have been made to put up
With all the shit, nameless people pileup.

You gave me a timetable and left my dreams in ruins.
You did everything for show and felt it in your bones.
You made your life all about mine,
And said it was all fine.

I wonder who you are trying to please.
You killed me with utmost ease.
By making your life all about mine,
And said it was all fine.

If you knew me better
Those words you wouldn't utter.
You were building a castle
And left me struggling in the hustle.

I knew you loved me,
And would kill for me.
But what were all that for,
When we placed our hearts miles afar?

I think I am at blame
That I could never be better than lame.
You deserve a better life.
You would've got it if I hadn't dropped that knife.
I made my life all about you,
And lived the matrix loop.